Growing Creative Kids

By Evelyn Petersen
Illustrated by Barb Tourtillotte

Totline® Publications
A Division of Frank Schaffer Publications, Inc.
Torrance, California

Dedicated with love to my children—Heather, Eric, Karin, and Kristin—and to their children and grandchildren. I hope that you and other readers of this book will always make it a priority to take time to enjoy activities with your children. It is through these experiences that we cherish and honor our childhood memories. It is during these moments that we pass on both our old and new family traditions. Keep making moments that will last for lifetimes. —E.P.

Managing Editor: Kathleen Cubley
Editor: Elizabeth McKinnon
Contributing Editors: Gayle Bittinger, Carol Gnojewski, Susan Hodges, Jean Warren
Copyeditor and Proofreader: Kris Fulsaas
Editorial Assistant: Durby Peterson
Graphic Designer (Interior): Sarah Ness
Graphic Designer (Cover): Brenda Mann Harrison
Production Manager: Melody Olney

ISBN: 1-57029-100-4

Library of Congress Catalog Card Number 96-61888
Printed in the United States of America
Published by Totline® Publications
Editorial Office: P.O. Box 2250
                       Everett, WA 98203
Business Office: 23740 Hawthorne Blvd.
                      Torrance, CA 90505

20 19 18 17 16 15 14 13 12 11 10 9 8 7 6 5 4 3

Introduction

When we understand what creativity really is, we can nurture it in our children every day.

Creativity is not a product, although it may result in something we can hear, touch, or see. Creativity is really a process of thinking and doing; it is a particular way of approaching life.

Creative thinkers are divergent thinkers. They know that there are many ways to solve a problem, not just one way. They know that there may be many correct answers to a question, not just one answer. When confronted with an obstacle, they think of new ways to work around it, "turning lemons into lemonade."

Creative thinkers enjoy playing with ideas and are not afraid to try them out.

When you see creativity in this light, you know that it is an important life skill for young children to learn. Creative thinking will help them in school. It will help them as adults when they are on the job and when they work with others. It will also help them when they need release from stress or a renewal of energy.

In this book, you will find many ideas you can use to encourage creativity in your own child. These ideas are grouped into nine chapters with titles such as "Creating With Natural Materials," "Creativity in the Kitchen" and "Creative Storytelling." All of the ideas are easy to put into practice right now, using materials that you probably have on hand.

As you look through *Growing Creative Kids*, you will see that it is not the music you play or the paintings on your wall that nurture creativity. It is the things you *do* with your young child that really nurture the seeds of creative and divergent thinking.

A WORD ABOUT SAFETY: The activities in *Growing Creative Kids* are appropriate for young children between the ages of 3 and 5. However, keep in mind that if a project calls for using small objects, an adult should supervise at all times to make sure that children do not put the objects in their mouth. It is recommended that you use art materials that are specifically labeled as safe for children unless the materials are to be used only by an adult.

Contents

Planting the Seeds of Creativity

Modeling Creativity

If you want your child to be a creative thinker, model creativity yourself. This doesn't mean that you have to be an artist or a dancer or a musician. It means showing your child that you are not afraid to try something new, whether it is playing with clay, testing a new recipe, making up silly songs or jokes, or improvising dance steps with him in the living room. Your child will learn about creativity by seeing you try new experiences and enjoy them.

Creativity is more caught than taught.

Saying "I Don't Know"

Finding out answers together can be fun.

Giving children answers whenever they ask questions can cut off other avenues of exploration. Every now and then, allow yourself and your child to experience not knowing the answer to a question. Don't be afraid to say, "I don't know." Say, "Let's try to find out," and then use resources such as library materials to search for the answer. Help your child understand that it is okay to not know about something and that it can be fun to try to discover answers together.

One Problem, Many Solutions

Exploring alternatives leads to creative thinking.

Whenever possible, show your child that there can be several ways to solve a problem and that all the solutions can be "right." For instance, consider different ways you could find out how tall your child is. You could use several types of rulers or measuring tapes; you could measure his height with a length of yarn, ribbon, or string; or you could compare his height to objects, furniture, or other people. You could also show your child that his height is the same measurement as his length when he is lying down, no matter what measuring tool you use. All the ways you could use to discover your child's height are different, and all of them are right.

Offering Choices

Learning to recognize and make choices is an important part of the creative process.

Each day, allow your child to make choices that she can handle. It is important that she experience the results of decision making and that she feel okay about her choices. Take time to plan and offer appropriate choices from which your child can learn. Here are some suggestions.

- At breakfast time, let her choose which of three nutritious cereals to eat.

- When it's time to get dressed, set out three or four shirts and let her choose one to wear.

- Show your child several seed packages and let her choose which seeds to plant in a garden or a flower pot.

Creative Problem Solving

Let your child experience creative problem solving at his developmental level. For instance, if he and a friend are having a problem during play, avoid jumping in and solving the problem for them. Instead, try following the steps below.

- ⊠ First, ask the children to stop and think about what they are doing and to tell each other how they feel.

- ⊠ Next, ask each of them to explain what the problem is.

- ⊠ Then, encourage the children to think of ways to solve the problem.

- ⊠ After several solutions are discussed, let them choose one and try it out.

- ⊠ Discuss whether the solution was successful. If it didn't work, encourage them to choose another one to try.

Children can learn how to resolve their own differences.

Listening

Listening carefully to your child says, "I think your ideas are important."

When your child is talking to you, listen—really listen— with your eyes, face, and whole body. Avoid "listening" while you are doing something else, even if you have to ask your child to wait a moment until you are finished with your task. Giving your full attention to your child tells her that you value her thinking and her ideas. When she knows this, she will do more thinking and come up with more ideas. As she does so, wait patiently for her to complete her thinking, and take care not to interrupt until she has had her say.

Asking Creative Questions

Learn how to ask "open" questions rather than "closed" ones. An open question is one that has many answers, all of which can be right, or that has an answer you don't already know. A closed question, on the other hand, has just one correct answer.

For example, if you and your child are looking at a table, a closed question would be, "What is this?" "What can you tell me about this table?" would be an open question. Your child could come up with many answers to the second question, such as, "It's round," "It's green," "It's where we eat," or "It's something to hide under."

Asking "What if?" questions is another way to stimulate your child's imagination. For instance, you might say, "What if we took this table outdoors? What could we do with it?" By using his imagination to move the table to a new place in his mind, your child is sure to come up with a whole new set of possibilities!

Questions that can have many different answers promote creative and divergent thinking.

No Copies, Please

The creative process is far more important than any product.

Let your child make her own drawings, paintings, clay sculptures, and other creations without giving her models or examples to copy. Providing a model not only squelches children's creative thinking, it also sets up an adult expectation for a product or an end result that they find impossible to reproduce. By the same token, avoid giving your child coloring books and telling her to "stay in the lines." Instead, encourage creativity by providing her with large, plain paper, along with crayons, markers, or paint, and the time and space to explore with them.

Creative Art Materials

Drawing and Scribbling

Crayons and markers are perfect open-ended art materials.

Open-ended art materials, such as crayons and markers, are those with which children can play and create any way they like. There is no predetermined result or "right" way to use them.

Every day, give your child some time and a special place to use crayons or markers of various kinds and large pieces of plain paper to draw or scribble on. Show your interest in his creations by describing what you see him doing and then asking questions. For instance, you might say, "You really like to use a lot of yellow. How do you feel about that color?" Or, "I see you are using lots of up and down lines and some round and curvy lines. Tell me about them."

Besides giving your child plain paper to draw on, try providing him with other materials such as colored construction paper, discarded computer paper, brown grocery bags, shirt cardboard, or old newspapers.

Making Collages

Making collages is a fun way to use up odds and ends that you just can't seem to throw away. Use an old shoebox to collect collage materials such as ribbon and fabric scraps, bottle caps, bread tags, stickers, buttons, plastic-foam peanuts, cotton swabs, cut-up drinking straws, yarn pieces, aluminum foil, and gift-wrap scraps.

Give your child stiff paper or recycled cardboard of any kind. Let her choose collage materials from the box and use glue from a small squeeze bottle to attach them to the paper or cardboard any way she wishes. Show her that one small drop of glue at a time works just fine. If you are concerned about glue drips, have your child keep her collage on a tray or a baking sheet while she works. Allow time for the glue to dry. Then display her creation on a shelf or a wall. Encourage your child to make more collages whenever she wishes.

Collage designs are interesting and fun for young children to create.

Painting

Nothing seems to make a child feel as creative and special as brushing vibrant, thick paint onto big pieces of paper.

Covering sheets of paper with bright colors of water-based paint develops creativity, self-esteem, and eye-hand coordination. Painting also stimulates the senses of sight, touch, and smell. Any kind of paper can be used—even recycled newspapers or paper bags—along with large paintbrushes and tempera paint.

For starters, buy red, blue, yellow, and white paint (available at art and crafts stores) and let your child experience the magic and pride of mixing his own orange, green, purple, or brown. Use a muffin tin to hold small amounts of the various colors of paint. Or put paint in margarine tubs, cut wide slots in the lids, and insert brushes. As your child removes the brushes from the tubs, he can press them against the sides of the slots to wipe off excess paint.

To extend the life of the paint and make cleanup easy, squeeze in drops of liquid dishwashing detergent. Have your child wear a large old shirt for a smock. Then place newspaper on your kitchen table and let him paint there, or have him work outside at a picnic table.

Fingerpainting

The best kind of paper to use for fingerpainting is white, shiny butcher paper, but any kind of large paper that is fairly nonabsorbent will work. Place a small amount of fingerpaint in the middle of the paper and let your child use her fingers, fists, and palms to move the paint around and create designs. Encourage her to continue working as long as she likes, creating lines, swirls, dots, and other patterns. Commercial fingerpaint is available at art and crafts stores, but here are a few suggestions for making your own.

Your child will love fingerpainting with the different kinds of paint you can provide at home.

- Add tempera paint to a small amount of liquid starch, thin wallpaper paste, or flour-and-water paste.

- Try condensed milk mixed with a small amount of tempera paint.

- Use hand lotion plain or mixed with a few drops of food coloring.

- Squirt unscented shaving cream directly onto a washable tabletop.

- For edible fingerpaint, use pudding, yogurt, or whipped cream.

Creating With Modeling Dough

Homemade modeling dough takes only a few minutes to make with ingredients you probably have on hand in your kitchen. Unlike commercial dough, it costs just a few pennies, and its natural ingredients ensure easy cleanup. Try the recipe on this page to make the dough. Keep some handy for you and your child to use daily at a table or on a baking sheet.

Also provide items for your child to use with the dough, such as a small rolling pin, a few small cake pans, and various safe kitchen gadgets. Encourage him to try rolling the dough, mashing it, flattening it, and pounding it. You will find that, besides being fun to touch and squeeze, the dough is a great stress reliever and that it offers many opportunities for your child to use language as he tells you what he is making.

Modeling Dough

- 2 cups flour
- 1½ cups water
- ½ cup salt
  Food coloring
- 1 Tbsp. vegetable oil
- 1 Tbsp. alum (available at drugstores)

Place flour in a large bowl. In a saucepan, heat water with salt. Stir to dissolve salt, and add drops of food coloring. As the water mixture begins to simmer, add oil and alum. Pour the mixture into the flour and stir well. As the dough cools, knead it until it becomes smooth. Store in an airtight container (no refrigeration needed).

Modeling dough allows your child to create whatever his imagination suggests.

Cornstarch Clay Fun

Use the recipe on this page to make a clay that is lusciously smooth, soft, and white. Let your child play with the clay and use it to make whatever she wishes. Allow her creations to air dry (they should do so without cracking). Then let her decorate her creations with tempera paint, if she likes.

Cornstarch Clay

  1 cup cornstarch

  2 cups baking soda

  1 ¼ cups cold water

In a saucepan, combine cornstarch, baking soda, and water. Cook over medium low heat, stirring constantly, until mixture thickens. When the mixture resembles thick mashed potatoes, it is done. Allow the clay to cool before use. It keeps well in an airtight plastic bag.

Your child will enjoy playing with this alternative to modeling dough.

Creating With Natural Materials

From Sandcastles to Mud Stew

Wet sand and mud are wonderful natural materials for encouraging creative play.

The joy of playing in wet sand or mud is something that most of us remember from our childhood. Find ways to help your child create such things as sandcastles, mud pies, and other similar inventions. If you don't have access to an outdoor sandbox or a dirt play area, just pour sand or soil into plastic dishpans. Let your child add a little water and mix well.

In the sandbox, place toys such as plastic containers of many sizes for molding, shells you have collected, or party toothpicks and golf tees for sandcastle flags and decorations. For encouraging mud play, give your child an old saucepan, some plastic bowls and spoons, and extra water in a small plastic pitcher. Encourage him to use the toys, along with grass, leaves, twigs, and seed pods, to make "mud stew." Model creativity—be sure to accept if he invites you to a pretend dinner!

Colored Sand Painting

Find some clean sand and pour it into several small margarine tubs or similar containers. Add drops of different-colored food coloring to each container, stir, and allow the sand to dry overnight. Place a piece of sturdy colored paper or white cardboard on an old baking sheet with sides, and let your child squeeze on glue to create designs. Help her sprinkle one color of sand over the glue and then lift the paper to allow the excess sand to fall into the baking sheet. Pour this sand back into its container. Then let your child add more glue and a different color of sand to her creation. Repeat this process until the sand painting is finished, then allow it to dry thoroughly.

For centuries, colored sand painting has been done by many cultures in many ways.

Water Play

For young children, playing creatively with water is a favorite pastime.

Young children enjoy the beauty of water and love using it in many ways for play, relaxation, and reducing stress. Be sure to allow your child time each day to play with water, whether it is in the bathtub or elsewhere.

Inside or outdoors, you can keep your child busy and happy with a plastic dishpan containing a few inches of water plus objects to pour with, fill, empty, float, and sink. Also, you can add a little liquid soap, give him a straw, and join him in blowing bubbles.

Or try this activity. On a table, set out several clear-plastic cups, each containing a straw, a few drops of liquid soap, and about an inch of water. (You will want to place the cups on paper towels to soak up any spills.) Blow through each straw to make bubbles that overflow the cup. Then help your child carefully squeeze drops of food coloring on top of the bubbles. The geometric designs you see will amaze you!

Snow and Ice Fun

Wintertime snow and ice invite creativity.

If you live in an area that has cold winter weather, you know that snow is a terrific open-ended play material. Young children love sliding, rolling, climbing, and falling down safely in snow. They also enjoy making snow people and snow angels.

For more wintertime fun, try something new—make an ice candle holder. On a day that is below freezing, let your child help you place a small or medium-sized bucket of water outdoors. Wait until the water is frozen at the top and around the sides, but not in the middle. (How long this takes will depend on how cold it is outdoors.)

Lay the bucket on its side and pour a kettle of very hot water over it. Briefly let the bucket cool, then let your child help slide the molded ice out of the bucket. Set the molded ice upright on the ground and you will have a beautiful candle holder that looks like fine crystal when a lighted votive candle is placed inside. Watch it with your child at night from a window. (Be sure to supervise children at all times around lighted candles.)

Nature Wall Decoration

Take your child for a walk in a park or a woodsy area, and bring along a paper bag. On the way, help him collect nature items such as moss, leaves, twigs, interesting small stones, miniature pine cones, and seeds.

Later, let your child make a plaster of Paris wall decoration with your findings. You will need an outdoor sandbox or a plastic dishpan with a layer of sand in the bottom. Make a shallow depression in the sand and in it let your child place favorite nature items from your walk, making sure that the "best" sides of the items are facing down. Mix a small batch of plaster of Paris, following the directions on the package, and gently pour it over the nature items. When the plaster is almost set, poke a hole in the decoration for inserting a hanger. Remove the decoration when the plaster has hardened, and brush off any loose sand.

Here's a creative way to use nature items for saving a memory or making a gift.

Dried Wood Creations

Every creation your child makes will be different and beautiful.

Walks in the woods or on the beach can yield findings of deadwood or driftwood in interesting shapes. Save these small pieces of wood in a box and add various mosses, stones, pine cones, shells, and other nature items your child finds. If you like, add a few dried straw flowers for color.

Place newspaper on a table. Let your child choose a piece of wood and an assortment of the other nature items from the box. First, have her glue the moss onto the wood piece. Then let her glue on the other items any way she wishes. Invite her to make as many dried wood creations as she likes.

Pet Rocks

A little love is all these creative pets require.

Many children want pets, but can't have them for various reasons. Children also love to collect stones and rocks. A creative way to combine these two ideas can be found in the following activity.

Take a walk with your child, bringing along a sturdy bag or box. Encourage him to collect several stones that fit in his hand and that feel good to the touch. When you get home, set out materials such as tempera paint and brushes, glue, scraps of fake fur, yarn pieces, and pipe cleaners. Let your child choose a stone and decorate it with the materials to make his own "Pet Rock" to carry around, talk to, and love. Encourage him to create more pets with his other stones, if he wishes.

More Fun With Natural Materials

Your child will enjoy discovering new ways to create with natural materials.

Below are just a few ideas for using natural materials in creative ways. You and your child are sure to come up with ideas of your own.

▓ Look for real clay in a riverbank or a shallow lake. Dig a little of it up and bring it home to use for modeling fun. Or purchase gray pottery clay from a hobby store for your child to use over and over again.

▓ Let your child gather nature items, such as stones, seed pods, twigs, and leaves, and then use them with blocks to create toy houses or towns.

▓ Show your child how to make a flower chain for a crown or a necklace. Poke a hole in a flower stem, thread the stem of another flower through the hole and pull it through until the flower head reaches the hole. Then poke a hole in the second flower stem and thread the stem of a third flower through it. Continue in the same manner until the chain is as long as you wish.

Creating With Familiar Materials

Goop

Whenever we use something in a new way, we model creative thinking.

Playing with Goop is a wonderfully messy activity that is best done outdoors, at least the first time. It shows children a new and different way of using a material that can be found in almost every kitchen cupboard.

To make Goop, just put ½ cup cornstarch into a small bowl and stir in tablespoons of water until the mixture looks wet, like glue, but feels dry to a light touch. Let your child put his hands into the bowl and play with the Goop, and encourage him to tell you how it feels. You can join in the fun, too. Show your child that if you keep the Goop moving as you handle it, it retains a shape, but if you hold it in your warm hand, it oozes.

Cardboard Tube Fun

Items you probably have on hand can be used in new ways just by applying a little imagination. For instance, find a cardboard tube such as a paper towel tube or a gift-wrap tube. Give the tube to your child and see how many ways the two of you can think of to use it. Below are a few suggestions to get you started.

A cardboard tube becomes much more than a throwaway when you use your imagination.

- Use it as a telescope.

- Turn it into a magic wand by gluing on sparkly decorations.

- Cut it into rounds and glue on decorations to make bracelets.

- Use it as a tunnel for tiny cars.

- Blow through it like a horn.

- Cut it into sections of different sizes and draw faces on the sections to make a family of puppets.

Invisible Ink Pictures

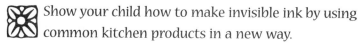

Children love the magic of drawing mystery pictures with invisible ink.

Show your child how to make invisible ink by using common kitchen products in a new way.

For the first method, let your child help you squeeze some lemon juice into a small bowl. Give him a piece of plain white paper and a cotton swab or a small brush. Have him dip the swab or brush into the juice and use it to draw a picture or a design on the paper. When the paper has dried, carefully hold it up to a hot light bulb and watch the picture become clear as the lemon juice turns brown. (This part of the activity is to be done only by an adult.)

A second method of making invisible ink also uses a common kitchen staple. Just stir 1 teaspoon baking soda with 2 teaspoons water until the soda dissolves. Paint with this mixture, then follow the same procedure described for the lemon juice, at left, to reveal mystery pictures.

Coat Hanger Creations

Creative thinking turns coat hangers into fun toys.

Almost everyone has a few wire coat hangers around the house. If you have extras, try turning them into toys for your child to play with. (Make sure that any sharp edges are covered with tape before giving the toys to your child.)

Make a safe bat that your child can use indoors with a crumpled newspaper ball. Bend a hanger into a oval shape. Find a clean pair of old pantyhose, stretch it over the wire oval, and wind the excess hose around the hook part of the hanger. Secure it in place with masking tape to make a handle.

For a different kind of toy, try fashioning a hanger into a giant bubble maker. Bend the hanger into a circle shape and wrap layers of masking tape around the hook part to form a handle. Pour some bubble solution into the bottom of a large shallow pan. (Use commercial solution or make your own by mixing together 2 quarts water, ¼ cup glycerin, and ¾ cup liquid dishwashing detergent.) Then take your child outdoors on a calm day. Help her dip the hanger into the solution and gently pull it through the air to make giant bubbles.

Junk Creations

Save odds and ends of materials such as cardboard tubes, parts of egg cartons, clean plastic-foam food trays, pipe cleaners, feathers from a duster, plastic straws, golf tees, cotton balls, twist ties, party plates and cups, pieces of nylon netting, old plastic flowers, and safe, unwanted items from your junk drawer. You can keep the materials in a plastic bag under your sink until you are ready to use them.

Surprise your child by spreading the "junk" out on a table and then working together to build a unique 3-D creation. Help him use a sturdy plastic-foam food tray or a disposable plastic plate as a base, and masking tape to attach and put together the pieces of junk you use. Encourage him to construct upward and outward, letting the creation evolve on its own. Later, you can take apart the construction, throw away the tape, and put the pieces back into the plastic bag to use again in a different and original way.

Creating with throwaways will make your child feel proud of "recycling."

Food Coloring Fun

A creative attitude turns food coloring into a fun art material.

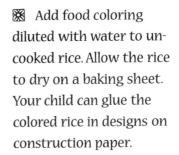 Here are a few suggestions for using food coloring in new ways. Perhaps you and your child will come up with more ideas.

※ Cook pasta shapes, such as macaroni, wheels, or bow ties, and tint them with food coloring. Allow the shapes to cool without rinsing them. Then let your child arrange the shapes on construction paper or cardboard any way she wishes to make a collage. (The unrinsed pasta will stick to the paper or cardboard, making glue unnecessary.)

※ Add food coloring diluted with water to uncooked rice. Allow the rice to dry on a baking sheet. Your child can glue the colored rice in designs on construction paper.

※ Mix different colors of food coloring with small amounts of water in small bowls. Help your child fold round coffee filters any way she wishes and then dip the corners into the different colors of food coloring to create a batik effect. Lay the filters flat to dry.

※ Fill a spray bottle with water and add red food coloring or tempera paint. On a winter day, go outside and spray your snow pink, as in the book *The Cat in the Hat Comes Back* by Dr. Seuss.

Marshmallow Constructions

Here's a tasty way to promote creative thinking.

On a table, set out toothpicks and some miniature marshmallows. Then invite your child to sit with you and do some creating. Show him how to use the toothpicks to connect the marshmallows in various ways. For instance, encourage him to try making geometric shapes such as squares and triangles. Or encourage him to create 3-D structures that can stand by themselves. When play time is over, help your child take apart his constructions and place the marshmallows in a bowl for snacking.

Graph a Snack

Food items become creative teaching aids at snacktime.

When you serve your child a snack that includes several food items, such as crackers of different shapes, you can create a new kind of learning experience by having her graph the snack before eating it.

Put a plain piece of paper on the table for a placemat. Draw lines on the paper from top to bottom to make columns. If the snack includes round, square, and triangular crackers, trace around a round cracker at the top of one column, a square cracker at the top of a second column, and a triangular cracker at the top of a third column.

Let your child sort her snack crackers by shape and then place them in the appropriate columns. If you like, talk about the concepts of "how many," "more or less," or "most and least" before your child enjoys her snack. This idea also works well with a snack mixture such as dry cereal, nuts, and pretzels.

Painting Surfaces

Painting on a variety of materials is both fun and creative.

When your child wants something to paint on, probably the first thing you reach for is plain white paper. To spark his creativity in a different way, gather other materials to paint on, give him paintbrushes and tempera paint, and let him experiment.

For instance, have him try painting on aluminum foil, cardboard, corrugated paper, scrap wallpaper, fabric scraps, stones, or bricks. Other surfaces to try are pieces of tree bark, scrap wood, old acoustical tiles, or vinyl tiles. Your child will learn that some surfaces need a lot more paint than others, and that the paint sticks better on some materials than on others.

More Uses for Familiar Materials

Seeing familiar materials used in new ways sparks creative thinking.

Be open to opportunities all around you to show your child creative new ways to use familiar materials. Here are just a few suggestions for you to consider.

⁂ Use baby food jars to make small terrariums for little plants your child has sprouted or moss that she has gathered.

⁂ Place an old shower curtain on the ground for a waterproof "blanket" when you and your child are having a picnic.

⁂ Cut brown paper grocery bags into squares, arrange them blank-side up, then staple the squares together to make a pad for drawing or coloring.

⁂ Let your child thread O-shaped cereal pieces on a 2-foot piece of string to make an edible necklace.

Creativity in the Kitchen

Creative Personalizing

Your child will love these creative ways of saying you care.

Keeping in mind that creativity often means doing something in a new way, you can give your child's sandwiches a "new look" by using a cookie cutter to make them heart-shaped. (This also boosts self-esteem by sending him a "You are special" message.)

Another way to do some creative personalizing is to form your child's initials with batter when you are cooking pancakes. Or use catsup or mustard to squeeze an "I love you," a heart shape, or his initials onto his hamburger.

Creative Toppings

Instead of serving your child plain hot cereal, or cereal with the same old topping, set out a few small bowls of toppings from which she can choose. For instance, try yogurt, applesauce, apple butter, fruit spread, chopped nuts, dates, raisins, fresh fruit, or granola. Your child may want to add just one topping, or she might choose to mix several of them on top of her cereal to experience some new and different tastes. Some of these toppings can also be used to add creative interest to cold cereals.

A simple food experience helps your child think and experiment creatively.

Think of other ways you can involve your child in adding new types of toppings to foods. What about peanut butter or coconut toppings for waffles, or a cream cheese mixture and chopped fresh veggies—chosen by your child—for a pizza?

Original Cake Decorating

This activity can provide creative fun with little mess.

Children of all ages love to decorate their own cakes, be it for birthdays or other special occasions. Obtain and keep on hand ingredients such as premade frosting, a variety of cake sprinkles, and several colors of decorative icing in squeezable tubes.

Spread out an old sheet or a shower curtain on the floor. In the middle of the sheet, place a frosted one-layer cake on a plate along with cake decorations and plastic knives and spoons. Let your child sit on the sheet and decorate the cake any way he wishes. If you like, let him add such items as animal crackers or chewy candy bears or worms. When it's time to clean up, just shake out the sheet and toss it into the washing machine.

Paintbrush Cookies

Help your child experience a new, creative way to paint.

With your child, make icebox sugar cookies, using a favorite recipe or one from a cookbook. (Any plain icebox cookies will work—the creative fun is in the cookie painting.) Place the cookies on a baking sheet.

Combine two egg yolks with 1 tablespoon water and pour the mixture into several cups of a muffin tin. Add drops of different-colored food coloring to the cups, using enough to make the colors deep and rich. Then let your child use small, clean paintbrushes or cotton swabs to paint the cookies with the egg yolk mixture any way she wishes. Bake the cookies according to your recipe directions. Enjoy!

Kitchen Stories

Delight your child by combining favorite tales with tasty treats.

There are many ways to creatively take your child's favorite stories into the kitchen. Below are a few you may wish to try.

"Goldilocks and the Three Bears" might inspire you to make porridge and retell the story.

"The Gingerbread Man" offers an opportunity to make gingerbread cookies and to discuss places the Gingerbread Man might run to from your home.

Dr. Seuss's book *Green Eggs and Ham* might motivate you to make green scrambled eggs (using food coloring) for breakfast or lunch.

Harry the Dog books by Gene Zion might suggest making peanut butter modeling dough and forming it into bone shapes for a snack. (Just mix equal parts peanut butter and powdered milk, sweeten with a little honey, and roll the finished shapes in wheat germ or graham cracker crumbs.)

Stone Soup

Check your local library for a copy of the folktale "Stone Soup" and read it to your child. Then arrange a time to make Stone Soup with your child. Your soup will be easy to prepare if you have planned ahead and saved soup stock, leftover bits of meat, and several kinds of vegetables.

Start by having your child find a smooth, hand-size stone. Scrub the stone thoroughly, boil it, and allow it to cool. Get out your soup pot and let your child add some water and the cooled stone. Using the story as a guide, help her add stock, meat, vegetables, and seasonings. Let the soup simmer as you read the story again.

Later, serve and eat the soup. Was it the stone or the ingredients you and your child added that made the soup taste so good? Let your child decide.

You and your child will have fun dramatizing this classic tale.

Kitchen Prints

Potato printing is fun and easy to do. To make a stamp, first slice a potato in half. Then use a pencil to draw the outline of a simple shape, such as a heart or a fish, on the cut surface of one of the potato halves. With a small, sharp knife, cut away the potato around the outside of the outline to create a raised shape.

Now all you need is a table covered with newspaper, some plain white paper, a shallow container, a sponge, and thick tempera paint. Place the sponge in the container and pour the paint over it. Your child can then press the potato stamp on the sponge and use it to make prints on the paper.

If you like, make several different potato stamps and set out red, yellow, and blue paint-covered sponges. Your child will be able to see new colors emerge when his prints overlap.

Other kitchen items your child can use to make prints are fruits, such as oranges, lemons, or apples, that have been cut in half. Or let him try printing with utensils such as a potato masher, a fork, a funnel, a slotted spatula, a cork, or small sponge pieces.

Making prints with kitchen materials is sure to bring out your child's creativity.

Different Doughnuts

Try this idea for using frozen biscuit dough in a new way. Pull the thawed biscuits apart and let your child create "doughnuts" by poking a big hole in the middle of each one.

In an electric frying pan, or a similar pan, heat vegetable oil for cooking the doughnuts. Let your child observe from a safe distance as you slide several doughnuts at a time into the oil with a long-handled, slotted spoon. When the doughnuts rise and start to brown at the edges, turn them over and allow them to finish cooking.

The doughnuts will be done very quickly. Test one to determine the cooking time needed in your pan.

Allow the doughnuts to cool. Then let your child shake them in a bag with sugar and cinnamon.

Here's a creative way of making a yummy treat for the whole family.

Creative Play

Time, Space, and Props

Nothing stretches your child's imagination as much as pretending.

To encourage your child's creativity, support his make-believe play and join with him in the fun whenever you can. Helping your child do pretend play is simple. All you really have to do is value it and consider it important. Then the rest is easy. Allow time and create some temporary space for pretend play when your child wants to do it, and provide props for him to use.

Many parents gather such props as dress-up skirts and pants, shoes, hats, jewelry, tote bags, scarves, old costumes, masks, and other odds and ends. They put them into a big box or a trunk. Everything is in one place, but what the child wants to use is often at the bottom.

An easier way of organizing pretend play props is to create several types of prop boxes in which the props for different kinds of play can be stored. For instance, you could use shoeboxes or cardboard cartons with lids to make prop boxes for playing dress-up, post office, restaurant, hospital, going to the beach, and so on. Keep the prop boxes stacked in a closet or in the garage.

More Props

It's easy to gather a few props and let your child create her own dramas.

With just a little effort, you can find props for various kinds of pretend play that your child is sure to enjoy. Below are a few suggestions.

For office play, let her use an old typewriter or a computer keyboard, paper, envelopes, rubber stamps, and a calculator or a telephone that no longer works.

Provide her with bandages, cotton balls, tongue depressors, and a man's white shirt for playing hospital. (Stuffed animals can serve as "patients.")

Stimulate car garage play by providing her with props such as toy cars and trucks, small tools, a flat bicycle inner tube, and an air pump.

For playing beauty salon, give her such props as towels, combs, a hairbrush, curlers, and a hand mirror.

Playing Store

This activity helps develop learning skills as well as creative thinking.

One of the easiest pretend play environments to create is a grocery store. In a corner of your kitchen, give your child small boxes and cans of food to arrange as he likes. Make paper money, add some real coins for change, and use a box or a silverware tray for a cash register. Let your child help make signs that tell the name of the store and some of the prices and "specials." Then give him paper or plastic bags for packing the groceries.

The fun thing about playing store is that your child can "sell" many items that you have in your home. For instance, using many of the props described above, he could sell shoes, hats, jewelry, or mittens and gloves.

Or you could help him create a toy store or even a pet store, using his own toys and stuffed animals for merchandise. Can your child think of other kinds of stores he could create?

Camping Play

Arrange a camping scene by setting up a real pup tent in the living room. Or make a tent by draping a sheet over a table. Small boxes can serve as chairs and tables, and pillows can be used for sleeping bags. Other props might include a water canteen, plastic dishes, a teakettle, a bucket, and a flashlight. For a pretend campfire, use cardboard tubes for logs and crumpled orange paper for flames.

As your child enjoys camping play, talk with her about how we do things outdoors, such as how we dress, cook meals, keep things clean, safely handle campfires, and act in the woods. Reinforce camping safety by asking "What if?" questions such as, "What if you saw some wild berries but didn't know what kind they were? Should you taste them? What if sparks from the fire got on your clothes? Can you show me how you would stop, drop, and roll?"

Camping is an activity that young children love to act out.

Fishing Fun

Pretend fishing is always fun for young children to do.

Set up a pretend fishing environment for your child by using empty boxes or a piece of furniture for a pier or a boat. Some props you can add are a life jacket, a hat with a visor, a fish net, a bucket, and a small tackle box.

For a fishing pole, attach one end of a string to a wooden dowel and tie a magnet to the other end. Cut fish shapes out of heavy paper and attach a jumbo metal paper clip to each one so that the fish can be "caught" with the magnet. An old fishing license or a handmade one makes another good prop. Join your child in his pretend play, if you wish. Ask him to tell you about the fish he is catching and what he is going to do with them.

Newspaper Pretending

Do pretend play with your child, not only to nurture creativity but also to have fun.

A sheet, some old newspapers, and a sense of humor are all you need for this pretend play game. Start by laying out the sheet on the floor for a "popcorn pan." Have your child help tear up the newspaper, crumple it into balls to represent popcorn kernels, and toss them onto the sheet. Pretend to heat up the oil in the "pan." With your child, hold on to the edges of the sheet, jiggling the popcorn as it gets hotter and hotter. Bounce the popcorn as it "pops" out everywhere.

Next, with your child, gather up the newspaper balls. Pretend that they are snowballs and have a great, safe snowball fight right in your own living room.

To end the game, have an old pillowcase handy. With your child, pick up the snowballs, put them into the pillowcase, and tie the pillowcase closed with string. Then have fun tossing this giant, light "ball" back and forth as long as you like.

Creative Storytelling

About Me Stories

Every storyteller brings part of him or herself to the story.

The stories that young children like best are those about themselves. Their favorite tales tell about when they were born, what they were like when they were younger, and what things they did as infants or toddlers. When you have told your child an "about me" story several times, he probably knows it well enough to tell it himself.

Encourage this kind of storytelling by looking together at photographs of your child, other family members, friends, and special events. Talk about the photos and ask questions for him to answer. When your child does this kind of storytelling, he is practicing the skills of creativity and language. Keep his interest high by sharing "about me" stories often.

Taped Stories

A good way to encourage storytelling is to tape record your child's voice as she makes up a story for you. You can ask questions or give cues to move the story along, but the real storyteller is your child. Creativity will be in high gear when the story told is a fantasy that your child makes up as she goes along.

To get a fantasy story started, you can ask "What if?" questions or use props such as stuffed animals or other toys. When your child finishes her story, you can both sit back and enjoy listening to the recording. You may wish to collect a number of her stories on tape to make a memento that she will cherish as a grownup.

Children love to hear themselves on tape when their stories are played back.

Picture Stories

When your child makes up stories about pictures, he is using his imagination and getting his creative wheels turning! Encourage this kind of storytelling by letting him help you look for interesting pictures in family or children's magazines. Cut out the pictures, glue them onto cardboard, and cover them with clear self-stick paper for durability. Keep the pictures handy in your child's book corner, by his bed, or in the car when you are traveling.

Whenever you have a moment, take out a picture and invite your child to describe the scene. Then ask him to tell you what he thinks might have happened before or after the scene. Are his stories about the pictures the same each time he tells them?

Imagining what might be happening in pictures stimulates your child's creativity.

Books Without Words

To promote storytelling, include wordless picture books in your child's own reading corner.

Ask the children's librarian at your local library to help you find a few wordless picture books. Choose one that interests your child, then invite her to sit with you. Open the book and go through the pages, asking her to tell you what she thinks is happening in the pictures. When you come to the end of the book, she will have told a "story."

There are many fine wordless picture books that will help your child become a creative storyteller. *Rosie's Walk* by Pat Hutchins and *Talking Without Words* by Marie Hall-Ets are just two of them.

Nursery Rhymes

Creative new twists can be added to nursery rhymes for everyone's enjoyment.

Most nursery rhymes, such as "Humpty Dumpty" or "Mary Had a Little Lamb," tell simple stories. Because they are rhymed stories, young children love them and are able to remember them well. Try changing a word in a familiar rhyme that you are reciting for your child and see how fast he tells you the right way to say it. ("No, Jack and Jill went to get some *water*, not ice cream!")

Or try changing the ending of a rhyme to start some giggles. ("Up above the world so high/Like a pancake in my eye!") Also, play charades with your child, acting out familiar rhymes, such as "Little Miss Muffet" or "Jack Be Nimble," and having the other person guess which rhymes they are.

Puppet Play

Another fine way to encourage your child's creative storytelling is to make puppets for her to use. You can create finger puppets by cutting the fingers off an old glove and adding faces to them. Or you can make a puppet out of a paper lunch sack by drawing on a face and gluing on yarn or cotton hair.

Or find an old sock, a worn-out footie, or an outgrown bedroom slipper to use for making a puppet. Gather materials such as fabric pieces, art foam and fake fur scraps, feathers from a duster, buttons, or sequins. Use the materials, along with glue and markers, to turn the sock, the footie, or the slipper into a puppet.

With your child, tell familiar or made-up stories, using your homemade puppets to dramatize the action. A good puppet story comes from the book *The Very Hungry Caterpillar* by Eric Carle. While telling the story, paper foods can be offered to the puppet for "eating."

Children like home-made puppets best.

Art Stories

Help your child learn that his words are important and that they can be written down as well as spoken.

Your child's artwork can become a springboard for creating original stories. When he is making a drawing or a painting, ask him to tell you about it. As he does so, write his words directly on his paper. You will find that as he talks about his picture, he probably will add more details, thus creating a longer and more interesting story.

Be sure to write your child's name on his stories and add the date. Then keep them in a special place where the two of you can enjoy "reading" them over and over again.

Experience Stories

Creating stories about special experiences helps keep memories alive.

When your child goes on a trip, goes fishing, or goes to an event such as a party or a fair—or even to the hospital— help her create an "experience story" about it. First, have her draw a picture illustrating the experience. Then, attach the picture to the top of a large piece of paper or posterboard, adding a few photos, if they are available.

Invite your child to talk about her experience. As she speaks, write her words on the paper beneath her picture. Encourage her to add details to her story by asking her questions. If an experience continues over several days, you might wish to record it on the pages of a scrapbook, helping your child create her own illustrated "storybook."

Me and d...
on the f...

My trip to the fair

Keeping a Journal

Starting a journal can lead to creative self-discovery.

By age 4 or 5, children can be encouraged to keep a personal journal, using any kind of notebook or scrapbook. A journal might start out as an "about me" book, containing dictated stories dealing with the family, a special pet, favorite colors and foods, fears, friends, and so on.

Then, parents can begin to encourage their child to dictate a few sentences each day for recording in the journal. These might tell what he liked best about the day or how he felt about something that happened.

If the child wants to skip "writing" in his journal for a day or two, that's fine; but it is important for parents to keep encouraging the regular habit of expressing thoughts and feelings in words. Children often "read" their journals and will try to do their own invented writing in them as well.

Arrow Story

For this story, you narrate the action and your child does the sound effects.

You and your child are sure to enjoy this creative participation story. First, cut an arrow shape out of cardboard. Show it to your child and explain that it is a volume controller. As you point the arrow upward, the sound grows loud; as you point it downward, the sound grows soft.

Then, start telling a story about a storm that comes and goes, letting your child do the sound effects. As she makes the sounds of wind, falling rain, and thunder, use the arrow to signal the wind growing stronger and stronger, the rain falling harder and harder, and the thunder booming louder and louder. (For added fun, switch a light on and off to represent lightning.)

Continue the story, using the arrow to indicate the dying sounds of the wind, rain, and thunder as the storm passes by and all is quiet again. Later, let your child help you create other stories about sounds that can be heard at places such as a farm, a zoo, or a busy street corner.

Creative Block Play

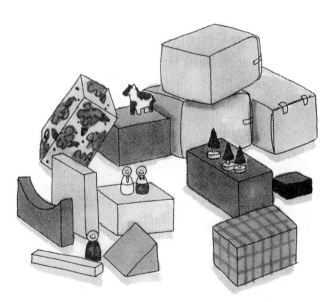

Family Block Play

Block play is even more fun when the whole family joins in.

Whenever children construct with blocks, they are doing a lot of creative thinking and problem solving. They are using an open-ended material to make their original ideas come to life.

Besides being a favorite activity for children, block play can also be a fun family activity. Because blocks are an open-ended material, there is no "right" or "wrong" way to use them. A person of any age can enjoy blocks. So, with your child, put blocks out on a table or on the floor some evening after dinner and gather everyone together. Build a tower, letting each person add one block at a time.

Your construction may evolve into a spaceship, a castle, a fancy house, or a high-rise. Encourage everyone to talk about the construction while you build, or make up a story about it. When all the blocks are used, or when the construction falls down, try building a new structure together.

Block Props

Adding props can make block play come alive.

Playing with blocks is even more fun when you can add props to the creation. If your child has miniature cars and trucks or small plastic people and animals, provide these as she constructs. You might also wish to enhance her block play by giving her some of the accessories below.

- scrap wood for bridges or roofs
- small stones, shells, or twigs for truck cargo
- tile or rug samples for floor covering
- cardboard signs for roads and stores
- evergreen twigs stuck into clay for trees
- Easter grass for barn hay
- cardboard boxes for garages or other buildings
- dollhouse furniture for house decorations
- odds and ends, such as thread spools, golf tees, pieces of rubber tubing, or plastic cups, for added details

As your child uses these props with her constructions, she will become like a puppeteer, creating stories and making her toy figures act them out.

Block Backdrop

This activity encourages beginning map skills.

You can add pizzazz to your child's block village or farm by giving him a backdrop to use for his play. For this purpose, find a large piece of white cardboard or an old shower curtain liner. Or use an old sheet, which has the advantage of being easy to fold up and store when not in use. Place the cardboard, the liner, or the sheet flat on the floor. Use permanent markers to draw on such things as roads, grass, bushes, gardens, and fields. Then let your child construct his block buildings on top of the scene any way he wishes.

Block Island

Block play can reinforce children's interest in the world around them.

If your child has a special interest such as islands, try helping her create one with blocks. Let your imaginations guide you. Make the island inside or outdoors. You might want to start by laying out a blue or a green sheet as a base for the blocks and providing your child with stones, sand, and small plastic boats. For greenery, you might give her real or artificial plants and flowers.

Your child can make pretend bridges from blocks, cardboard, or large pieces of plastic foam. You can even help her create a suspension bridge by draping string from the bridge towers and attaching it with masking tape. Looking at magazine pictures of islands or reading library books about them are good follow-up activities.

Big, Big Blocks

Young children feel really strong and smart when they can play safely with large, lightweight blocks. Sometimes they just want to build a little "house" or a "cave" around themselves and then burst out of it by knocking down the blocks.

You can make your own big, hollow blocks out of half-gallon milk cartons. For one block, cut the triangular tops off two cartons and fit one carton inside the other, as shown in the illustration. If you ask friends and relatives to help you save cartons, your child will soon have enough blocks to do lots of building. Cover the blocks with colorful self-stick paper, if you wish.

Another easy way to make big, lightweight blocks is to stuff brown paper grocery bags with crumpled newspaper and then close them with tape.

Your homemade blocks will make big block play especially fun.

Dramatic Play

Block structures are perfect for stimulating creative dramatic play.

When you have a generous supply of big, lightweight blocks (see opposite page), your child can use them to build a "stage set" in which she is the actor, using her imagination to make up her own play. You can provide dress-up clothes or props to add to the creative thinking and fun.

For instance, the blocks could become an office (add an old typewriter, junk mail, a calculator, etc.); a grocery store (add small cans, food boxes, play money, etc.); a hospital (add dolls, a stethoscope, bandages, etc.); or a boat (add life jackets, fishing poles, a net, etc.). Encourage your child to come up with ideas of her own—then on with the play!

Acting Out Stories

Provide both props and praise, and keep your camera handy.

Reinforce your child's language and creative thinking skills by letting him use big, lightweight blocks (see page 82) for acting out favorite stories. For instance, he could make the Three Bears' house with the blocks, or a train from Watty Piper's *The Little Engine That Could*. Give him appropriate props, then encourage him to act out the stories as you read or tell them.

You can also make up your own stories for your child to act out. He could use the blocks to build a boat for a story about sailing to a magical country. Or he could build a block spaceship for a story about a trip to the moon. This kind of dramatic play gives your child the opportunity to use blocks in positive, creative ways.

Block Memory Games

You can use small blocks in a new way to help your child practice her memory skills. First, arrange several blocks of different colors and shapes on a tray or a table. After your child has looked carefully at the arrangement, ask her to close her eyes. Then, take away one of the blocks. Have your child open her eyes and try to guess which one you removed. For the next round of the game, replace the block, close your own eyes, and let your child choose a block to remove. Continue playing in the same manner as long as you wish.

Here's another memory game that is a little like Hide-and-Seek. Hide several blocks in a room, setting aside an exact set of matching blocks. Select one or two blocks from this set and give them to your child. Have her take the blocks around the room, find their hidden matches, and then bring them back to you.

Using blocks in new ways fosters creativity.

Creativity Through Music and Dance

Kitchen Band

When children experiment with sounds, they are actually creating their own music.

Take a new look at the various objects in your kitchen drawers and cupboards—you may be surprised by the kinds of musical sounds that can be created with them. For instance, shake a tea ball for a tinkling sound or use tongs for a clicking sound. Or try making sounds by rolling the working end of wire whisk across a table, cranking an old hand-held egg beater, or banging on a pan lid with a wooden spoon.

Then model creativity by taking time to use these music makers with your child. You can turn on some music to accompany your "kitchen band" instruments. Or, on a nice day, you can invite others to join the two of you and have an outdoor parade.

Body Band

You will be nurturing creative thinking when you help your child make music in different ways.

Young children can be very creative when they are encouraged to make sounds with their bodies, using no musical instruments or props. When your child has friends over, take a few minutes to show them how to create a "body band." Ask them to demonstrate different sounds they can make. They will likely stamp their feet, try to snap their fingers, clap their hands, click their tongues, try to whistle, slap their thighs, and come up with a variety of sounds you never thought possible. Turn on some music or sing a simple song and let the "body band" play along. The children will love it, and so will you!

Homemade Drum Set

You will be amazed at how easily you can put together a homemade set of drums for your child. Just look in your kitchen cupboards for unopened or empty cans and cylindrical containers of different sizes. They can be as small as juice cans, coffee cans, or oatmeal boxes, or as large as overturned buckets or wastebaskets.

Give your child two wooden spoons for drumsticks. Or make your own drumsticks by inserting the ends of two short dowels into corks. Then set up the containers near some music and let your child play along. Show him that tall cans make sounds different from short cans, and that sounds also differ due to the types of containers or what is in them.

If you like, you and your child can make a small drum out of a coffee can that is open at both ends. Cut two pieces of an old inner tube into circles that are larger than the ends of the can. Punch holes around the edges of the rubber circles and use rawhide strips or shoe laces to lace these coverings over the two can ends.

Parents don't have to buy instruments to foster musical creativity.

More Homemade Instruments

All sorts of musical instruments can be made from common materials found in your home.

The most important way for parents to encourage creativity with music is to show their children that they themselves value and enjoy it. Take time to make music with your child. Also, encourage interest by constructing one or more of the simple instruments below.

Guitar—Find a sturdy plastic container or wooden box. Stretch one or two strong rubber bands around the open container and pluck the "strings" to make sounds.

Tambourine—Punch holes around the edge of a disposable plastic plate. Use pipe cleaners threaded through the holes to attach small metal washers or jingle bells.

Shakers—Fill empty film containers with such materials as sand, rice, popcorn kernels, dried beans, coins, or pebbles. Fasten the lids on tightly and reinforce them with strong tape.

Kazoo—Cover one end of a cardboard toilet tissue tube with waxed paper, securing it with a rubber band. Poke a hole near the other end of the tube. To play, hum into the open end.

Musical Movement Motivators

Homemade props add to the joy of moving to music.

Many children like to use some kind of prop when they move or dance to music. It helps them move with the flow and makes them feel less self-conscious. Such props are easily found in most homes. Below are some examples.

If you have an old, worn sheet, tear it into strips about 1 to 2 feet wide. You and your child can use the strips as "towels" and pretend that you are drying off after a shower as you move to music. Call it "towel dancing."

Find some old scarves or ribbons to hold onto and wave in the air as you and your child dance. If you need extras, check local thrift stores. They usually have lots of scarves and ribbons that cost next to nothing.

Crepe-paper streamers also work well as movement props. They are inexpensive, colorful, and easy to roll up and store.

Pompom Fun

You can make colorful pompoms to use with your child for dancing and waving to the beat of the music. Find cardboard tubes such as toilet tissue tubes or paper towel tubes. Cut crepe-paper streamers to any length you wish. Then cut each strip in half lengthwise. Tape a handful of these streamers inside each of the cardboard tubes, which will serve as handles for the pompoms. If you wish, cover the tubes with aluminum foil to add strength and sparkle.

Give your child two and take two yourself. Turn on some music. Then play the role of leader and have your child copy your movements as you dance and shake your pompoms up and down, back and forth, in front of you, and behind you. When the music ends, change places and let your child be the pompom leader.

Pompoms are perfect props to use for dancing to music.

Title Index

Totline
Publications

Teacher Books

BEST OF TOTLINE® SERIES
Totline Magazine's best ideas.
Best of Totline
Best of Totline Parent Flyers

BUSY BEES SERIES
Seasonal ideas for twos and threes.
Busy Bees—Fall
Busy Bees—Winter
Busy Bees—Spring
Busy Bees—Summer

CELEBRATIONS SERIES
Early learning through celebrations.
Small World Celebrations
Special Day Celebrations
Great Big Holiday Celebrations
Celebrating Likes and Differences

EXPLORING SERIES
Versatile, hands-on learning.
Exploring Sand
Exploring Water
Exploring Wood

FOUR SEASONS
Active learning through the year.
Four Seasons—Art
Four Seasons—Math
Four Seasons—Movement
Four Seasons—Science

GREAT BIG THEMES SERIES
Giant units designed around a theme.
Space • Zoo • Circus

KINDERSTATION SERIES
Learning centers for learning with language, art, and math.
Calculation Station
Communication Station
Creation Station
Investigation Station

LEARNING & CARING ABOUT
Teach children about their world.
Our World • Our Town

MIX & MATCH PATTERNS
Simple patterns to save time!
Animal Patterns
Everyday Patterns
Holiday Patterns
Nature Patterns

1•2•3 SERIES
Open-ended learning.
1•2•3 Art
1•2•3 Blocks
1•2•3 Games
1•2•3 Colors
1•2•3 Puppets
1•2•3 Reading & Writing
1•2•3 Rhymes, Stories & Songs
1•2•3 Math
1•2•3 Science
1•2•3 Shapes

1001 SERIES
Super reference books.
1001 Teaching Props
1001 Teaching Tips
1001 Rhymes & Fingerplays

PIGGYBACK® SONG BOOKS
New lyrics sung to the tunes of childhood favorites!
Piggyback Songs
More Piggyback Songs
Piggyback Songs for Infants and Toddlers
Holiday Piggyback Songs
Animal Piggyback Songs
Piggyback Songs for School
Piggyback Songs to Sign
Spanish Piggyback Songs
More Piggyback Songs for School

PROBLEM SOLVING SAFARI
Teaching problem solving skills.
Problem Solving—Art
Problem Solving—Blocks
Problem Solving—Dramatic Play
Problem Solving—Manipulatives
Problem Solving—Outdoors
Problem Solving—Science

REPRODUCIBLE RHYMES
Make-and-take books for emergent readers.
Alphabet Rhymes
Object Rhymes

SNACKS SERIES
Nutrition combines with learning.
Super Snacks • Healthy Snacks
Teaching Snacks • Multicultural Snacks

TERRIFIC TIPS
Handy resources full of valuable tips.
Terrific Tips for Directors
Terrific Tips for Toddler Teachers
Terrific Tips for Preschool Teachers

THEME-A-SAURUS® SERIES
Classroom-tested, instant themes.
Theme-A-Saurus
Theme-A-Saurus II
Toddler Theme-A-Saurus
Alphabet Theme-A-Saurus
Nursery Rhyme Theme-A-Saurus
Storytime Theme-A-Saurus
Multisensory Theme-A-Saurus

TODDLER SERIES
Great for working with 18 mos–3 yrs.
Playtime Props for Toddlers
Toddler Art

Tot-Mobiles
Unique sets of die-cut mobiles for punching out and easy assembly.
Animals & Toys
Beginning Concepts
Four Seasons

Puzzles & Posters

PUZZLES
Kids Celebrate the Alphabet
Kids Celebrate Numbers
African Adventure
Underwater Adventure
Bear Hugs 4-in-1 Puzzle Set
Busy Bees 4-in-1 Puzzle Set

POSTERS
We Work and Play Together
Bear Hugs Health Posters
Busy Bees Area Posters
Reminder Posters

Parent Books

A YEAR OF FUN SERIES
Age-specific books for parenting.
Just for Babies
Just for Ones
Just for Twos
Just for Threes
Just for Fours
Just for Fives

BEGINNING FUN WITH ART
Introduce your child to art fun.
Craft Sticks • Crayons • Felt
Glue • Paint • Paper Shapes
Modeling Dough • Tissue Paper
Scissors • Rubber Stamps
Stickers • Yarn

BEGINNING FUN WITH SCIENCE
Spark your child's interest in science.
Bugs & Butterflies • Plants & Flowers
Magnets • Rainbows & Colors
Sand & Shells • Water & Bubbles

KIDS CELEBRATE SERIES
Delightful stories with related activity ideas, snacks, and songs.
Kids Celebrate the Alphabet
Kids Celebrate Numbers

LEARN WITH PIGGYBACK® SONGS
Captivating music with age-appropriate themes help children learn.
Songs & Games for Babies
Songs & Games for Toddlers
Songs & Games for Threes
Songs & Games for Fours
Sing a Song of Letters
Sing a Song of Animals
Sing a Song of Colors
Sing a Song of Holidays
Sing a Song of Me
Sing a Song of Nature
Sing a Song of Numbers

LEARN WITH STICKERS
Beginning workbook and first reader with 100-plus stickers.
Balloons • Birds • Bows • Bugs
Butterflies • Buttons • Eggs • Flags
Flowers • Hearts • Leaves • Mittens

LEARNING EVERYWHERE
Discover teaching opportunities everywhere you go.
Teaching House
Teaching Trips
Teaching Town

PLAY AND LEARN
Activities for learning through play the Totline way.
Blocks • Instruments • Kitchen
Gadgets • Paper • Puppets • Puzzles

SEEDS FOR SUCCESS
Ideas to help children develop essential life skills for future success.
Growing Creative Kids
Growing Happy Kids
Growing Responsible Kids
Growing Thinking Kids

TIME TO LEARN
Ideas for hands-on learning.
Colors • Letters • Measuring
Numbers • Science • Shapes
Matching and Sorting • New Words
Cutting and Pasting
Drawing and Writing • Listening
Taking Care of Myself

Puppet Pals
These instant puppets fit on craft sticks, pencils or straws for language props, rewards, and more!
Children's Favorites • The Three Bears
Nursery Rhymes • Old MacDonald
More Nursery Rhymes • Three Little Pigs • Three Billy Goats Gruff
Little Red Riding Hood